Your Creative Process

Unleash Your Creative Potential: Empowering Minds, Inspiring Creativity

KELLY BARKER

First published by Ultimate World Publishing 2024
Copyright © 2024 Kelly Barker

ISBN

Paperback: 978-1-923255-26-5
Ebook: 978-1-923255-27-2

Kelly Barker has asserted her rights under the Copyright, Designs and Patents Act 1988 to be identified as the author of this work. The information in this book is based on the author's experiences and opinions. The publisher specifically disclaims responsibility for any adverse consequences which may result from use of the information contained herein. Permission to use information has been sought by the author. Any breaches will be rectified in further editions of the book.

All rights reserved. No part of this publication may be reproduced, stored in or introduced into a retrieval system, or transmitted in any form, or by any means (electronic, mechanical, photocopying, recording or otherwise) without the prior written permission of the author. Any person who does any unauthorised act in relation to this publication may be liable to criminal prosecution and civil claims for damages. Enquiries should be made through the publisher.

Cover design: Ultimate World Publishing
Layout and typesetting: Ultimate World Publishing
Editor: Vanessa McKay

Ultimate World Publishing
Diamond Creek,
Victoria Australia 3089
www.writeabook.com.au

Testimonials

"Kelly's workshop on 'Your Creative Process' is one of those workshops that both inspires and educates. Being in person, you have the opportunity to put voice and clarity to your thoughts in a supportive, enlivened and enriched group of folks who are on the same journey. To have a group environment that you can bounce ideas off and practice processes is really awesome. To understand the process that Kelly works through for her art is inspirational AND interesting. We all work differently and are at different levels and places in our art path but the information received and taught by Kelly is relevant to any form of art at any stage. It's amazing actually how many times processes and information bought up in those few hours have just popped into my mind well after the workshop was over....once taught and tried, these processes really work. Truly a great investment!"

Sharon R

Your Creative Process

"This workshop offers practical, easy exercises to unlock creativity. I came feeling quite stagnant with my work and taking out my camera felt like 'work'. I love how this workshop has motivated me to go out and search for intriguing subjects to photograph and brought back the feeling of excitement to my photography, looking at new ways to see the world and to tell stories in a different way."

Anthea K

Dedication

This book is a tribute to the two most extraordinary people in my life: my beloved mum and dad. To Mum and Dad, your presence has been the steadfast pillar of support and the embodiment of a love that one often only encounters in the pages of fiction. Your unwavering belief in my abilities, even during moments of self-doubt, has served as my bedrock. Whether my ideas were rational, whimsical, or seemingly insane, you've stood by me with unwavering support. I couldn't have asked for better parents, and I am eternally grateful for everything you've done for me. With a heart bursting with love and a reverence that transcends words, this book is dedicated to you both.

Ian, Bethany, and Zachary, my cherished little family. You fill my days with inspiration and continually encourage me to evolve into the

Your Creative Process

best version of myself. Your unwavering belief in me fuels my determination to pursue authenticity and strive to meet the lofty expectations you hold for me. Your steadfast support and unconditional faith mean the world to me, and I am profoundly grateful for all that you do. I owe every success to your love and encouragement.

To my dear brothers and your families, sharing our journey from childhood to adulthood has been a ride dappled with cherished memories and transformative experiences. Though not without our share of disagreements and debates, the bond we share remains unbreakable. I am deeply grateful for the love and support you and your families have consistently shown me, and I hold each of you dear to my heart.

Karen, from the depths of my heart, I extend my deepest gratitude to you. You're not just a friend; you're like a sister to me. Your unwavering support, encouragement, and belief in me holds immeasurable value. Your daily inspiration fuels my spirit, and from the inception of this journey, you've been by my side, offering guidance and support every step of the way. Your role as a sounding board has been monumental, and I owe the fruition of this endeavour to your invaluable contributions.

Dedication

To Des, Sam and Shannon. I want to express my heartfelt gratitude for your editing and invaluable enhancements to this book. Your feedback and input have not only bolstered my confidence but also illuminated the path of this journey with clarity and authenticity. Your opinions are of utmost importance to me, and I deeply appreciate the time and effort you've dedicated to providing them.

Contents

Testimonials	iii
Dedication	v
Chapter 1: Creativity. What is it? Why do we need it?	1
Chapter 2: About Me	7
Chapter 3: Why do people consider themselves uncreative?	13
Chapter 4: Empowering your creativity	23
Chapter 5: Creativity Training - Process One	31
Chapter 6: Creativity Training - Process Two	41
Chapter 7: Creativity Training - Process Three	51
Chapter 8: Creativity Training - Process Four	61
Chapter 9: Creativity Training - Process Five	71
Chapter 10: Creativity Training - Process Six	81
Chapter 11: Things to remember throughout the process	89
Chapter 12: So where to from here?	93
About The Author	97
More Testimonials	99
Creative Learning Paths	101

Chapter 1

Creativity. What is it? Why do we need it?

Creativity. What is it? Why do we need it?

Creativity.... What is it?

The Oxford Learners Dictionary in June 2024 defines creativity as, "the use of skill and imagination to produce something new or to produce art."

Creativity is a complex cognitive process that involves generating ideas, solutions, or expressions. It's a fundamental aspect of humanity and intelligence and plays a crucial role in so many areas of expertise. Creativity is the generation of novel ideas, solutions, or interpretations that are valuable or meaningful. It encompasses the ability to think divergently, make connections between seemingly unrelated concepts, and produce original and innovative outcomes. What does all that truly mean? It means that we use creativity EVERY DAY, in everyday life, in everyday decisions, in everyday relationships. It is a part of who we all are.

The generation of ideas, solutions, or interpretations can manifest in various forms, such as new combinations of existing elements, entirely unique concepts, or fresh perspectives on familiar topics. Idea generation also carries a sense of value or meaning. Whether it's solving a problem, inspiring emotions, sparking intellectual curiosity, or challenging established norms, creative ideas and interpretations often resonate with individuals and communities in profound ways.

Creativity is the ability to think convergently and also divergently. Mixing both involves exploring multiple possibilities and perspectives. Creative individuals often exhibit a willingness to break free from conventional thinking patterns and explore unconventional avenues. This book will bring a sense of strategy to these thinking patterns that can be taught and nurtured in each of us. I use a structure and planned process that removes the overwhelm. **Every single one of us has the ability to be creative and to think creatively.**

So why is creativity a basic human function?

Creativity is a fundamental aspect of human cognition and behaviour that enhances our ability to adapt, innovate, communicate, and thrive. By nurturing and embracing creativity, we can unlock our full potential and contribute to positive change in both our own lives and in the world around us.

From simple everyday actions to the extreme in creativity, the process principles are still relevant. By understanding and embracing these principles, we can cultivate our own creativity and apply it effectively in various aspects of our lives, from

Creativity. What is it? Why do we need it?

problem-solving and self-expression to innovation, personal growth and trauma release, to business solutions and even to relationship growth.

Chapter 2

About Me

About Me

Allow me to confide in you, a personal development. During my formative years, I often perceived myself as slightly unconventional, feeling that my thought processes diverged from the norm. This awareness made me somewhat self-conscious. One of my enduring habits has been to explore alternative viewpoints, both literally and metaphorically. When everyone's attention was fixed in one direction, I instinctively turned mine in the opposite direction, curious about what might be overlooked. Similarly, when presented with an argument, I've consistently adopted the role of devil's advocate, relishing the opportunity to delve into opposing perspectives. Paradoxically, despite this inclination, I wouldn't classify myself as rebellious; outwardly, I tend to conform to societal expectations. As an introvert, I find solace in the background, yet internally, I seek the debate and thrive on looking at all facets of any situation.

In more recent years, I have come to accept this, embrace it, and even love it.

An enduring fascination with art, design and photography has been a driving force in my life journey. Throughout high school, I eagerly immersed myself in as many art based electives that my schedule could accommodate. Upon entering tertiary studies, I delved into graphic

Your Creative Process

design and multimedia, ultimately finding my calling in photography. The allure of the studio environment, painting with light, and creating compositions, captivated me. The passion for the creative process blossomed further as I delved into the post processing techniques, revelling in the ability to craft surreal ideas by combining elements from separate photographs. It was during this exploration that my photographic artwork took shape, sparking a profound interest in the workings of the human mind and the genesis of creating ideas. As I honed my craft, I became intrigued by the cognitive process underlying creativity, observing how ideas germinated and problems were solved with my mind. This curiosity spurred me to delve into the documented methods of creative thinking, seeking ways to train and manipulate my brain to tap into its subconscious depths. I realised that my creative process draws from both the left and right brain and that, as a result, my methodology had evolved to incorporate strategic and logical elements (left brain) to complement the creative and artistic (right brain).

As my photographic endeavours gained public recognition, I began fielding enquiries about the genesis of my ideas and the creative process that I used to bring these ideas to fruition. Inspired by these questions, I embarked on the development

About Me

of a book and workshop series centered on the intricacies of the creative journey. My aim was to illuminate the pathways to inspiration and innovation for people of any skill level by simplifying and documenting my process. Utilising my ability to incorporate both left and right brain thinking to articulate an approach that can be embraced by individuals of any creative level.

Chapter 3

Why do people consider themselves uncreative?

Why do people consider themselves uncreative?

But I don't have a creative or weird and wacky mind you say?

A recent global study conducted by Adobe revealed that 75% of individuals feel they're falling short of their creative capabilities.

Why do people believe they aren't creative?

Misconceptions about creativity. One common misconception is the belief that creativity is synonymous only with artistic or musical ability. While it's true that artists and musicians often demonstrate remarkable creative prowess, creativity is not limited to these domains. In reality, creativity permeates every facet of human endeavour, from scientific exploration and technological innovation to business strategy and everyday problem-solving. Indeed, at its core, creativity encompasses the ability to generate novel ideas, devise innovative solutions, and think outside the box—qualities that are invaluable across diverse fields and disciplines.

Unfortunately, this narrow perception of creativity can lead individuals who do not see themselves as particularly artistic or musical to doubt their own creative abilities. They may erroneously conclude that creativity is a talent reserved for a select few, failing to recognise the myriad ways in which it can manifest in their own lives. Consequently,

Your Creative Process

they may overlook opportunities to tap into their creative potential and contribute original insights and ideas into their personal and professional endeavours.

In truth, creativity is a multifaceted and inclusive phenomenon that knows no bounds. Whether it's devising a new business strategy, designing an innovative product, or finding a creative solution to a complex problem, everyone possesses the capacity for creative thinking. By broadening our understanding of creativity and embracing its diverse manifestations, we can cultivate a culture that celebrates and nurtures creative expression in all its forms, empowering individuals to unlock their full creative potential and make meaningful contributions to the world around them

Fear of failure. The fear of failure is a formidable barrier that many individuals encounter on their creative journey. Creativity inherently involves taking risks, venturing into uncharted territory, and embracing the unknown. However, for some people, the prospect of failure looms large, casting a shadow over their willingness to explore and experiment. This fear can stem from various sources, including experiences of criticism or rejection, societal pressure to adhere to norms and expectations, parental or upbringing expectations, or simply a lack of

Why do people consider themselves uncreative?

confidence in their own ability. At its core, the fear of failure is rooted in a deep-seated aversion to judgment, criticism, or disappointment. People may worry that their creative ideas will be met with ridicule or disdain, that their efforts will fall short of expectations, or that they will be unable to live up to self-imposed standards of success. These apprehensions can paralyse individuals, leading them to shy away from creative pursuits altogether, or to play it safe by sticking to familiar territory and avoiding anything that might challenge their comfort zone. The fear of failure can be exacerbated by a culture that places undue emphasis on perfectionism and achievement. In a society that often equates success with flawless performance and unblemished outcomes, the fear of falling short can become overwhelming, driving individuals to adopt a risk-averse mindset and avoid any situation where failure is a possibility.

However, it's important to recognise that failure is an inherent part of the creative process—and indeed, of life itself. Failure is not a sign of inadequacy or incompetence but an opportunity for growth, learning, and resilience. By reframing failure as a natural and necessary part of the journey toward innovation and discovery, individuals can cultivate a more positive attitude toward risk-taking and experimentation. They can learn to embrace failure as a stepping stone to success, recognising that each setback brings valuable lessons and insights that can inform future endeavours.

Overcoming the fear of failure requires courage, perseverance, and a willingness to confront discomfort head-on. It involves reframing negative beliefs or self-limiting beliefs, cultivating self-compassion and resilience, and embracing a growth mindset that welcomes challenges and setbacks as opportunities for growth. By fostering a supportive environment that encourages risk-taking and celebrates creativity in all its forms, individuals can overcome the fear of failure and unleash their full creative potential.

Lack of confidence. The lack of confidence is a pervasive obstacle that can hinder individuals from realizing their creative potential. Even when they possess innovative ideas or concepts, self-doubt can cripple their belief in their ability to bring those ideas to fruition. This lack of confidence may stem from various factors, including perceived inadequacies in skills or knowledge, experiences of failure or rejection, or comparisons with others who appear more accomplished.

One of the primary contributors to the lack of confidence is a perceived deficiency in skills or expertise. Individuals may doubt their capacity

Why do people consider themselves uncreative?

to execute their creative vision effectively, fearing that their technical abilities may fall short of the demands of their chosen pursuit. This insecurity can be particularly acute in fields where mastery of specific tools or techniques is required, such as graphic design, writing, or music composition. Individuals may wrestle with imposter syndrome—a pervasive feeling of being a fraud or undeserving of success. They may downplay their achievements, attributing them to luck or circumstance rather than acknowledging their own talents and efforts. Not celebrating or recognising the achievements they have on their journey. Often people focus on the lessons learnt as failures, rather than growth, and miss the opportunity to see how far they have come from where they started. This self-doubt can undermine their confidence and erode their motivation to pursue creative endeavours. The fear of failure plays a significant role in perpetuating the lack of confidence. Individuals may worry that their efforts will not meet their own expectations or the expectations of others, leading them to question their ability to succeed. This fear of falling short can be paralysing, causing individuals to procrastinate or avoid taking risks that are essential for creative growth.

Ultimately, building confidence is a gradual process that requires patience, perseverance, and self-compassion. By nurturing a belief in their own potential and embracing a growth mindset, individuals can overcome self-doubt and unlock their full creative capabilities.

Comparison to others. Comparing oneself to others can often lead to feelings of inadequacy or a sense of lacking. Creativity is not an inherent fixed trait that some individuals possess, while others do not. It is something everyone is born with but may lack the skills to fully access their own depths of creativity. Access can be nurtured, developed and enhanced through practice and experimentation. Each person brings a unique set of experiences, knowledge, and thought processes to the table, shaping how they approach problems and generate solutions. Individuals are likely to tackle the same problem in different ways, yielding a diverse range of outcomes. Various factors influence how individuals approach problem-solving. These include background and experience, personality and cognitive style, problem-solving skills, and pre-existing beliefs. Recognising and embracing these individual differences is key to fostering a culture of creativity and innovations.

There are many approaches to problem-solving, each suited to different situations and preferences. An analytical approach involves breaking down

Why do people consider themselves uncreative?

a problem into smaller, more manageable parts and analysing each component independently. For instance, solving a Sudoku puzzle entails scrutinizing each row, column, and square methodically. A trial-and-error approach involves experimenting with different solutions until the optimal outcome is achieved, akin to fitting pieces together in a jigsaw puzzle. Alternatively, a visual approach entails identifying patterns, common themes, colours, or symmetries to uncover solutions, such as grouping together similarly coloured pieces in a jigsaw puzzle. Whether one leans towards an analytical, trial-and-error, or visual thinking style, it's essential to cultivate flexibility and adaptability in problem-solving. Embracing each approach and stepping outside of one's comfort zone can lead to novel insights and innovative solutions. As a facilitator, I'm here to support individuals in harnessing their unique thinking styles and exploring new avenues of creativity.

Time restraints. The scarcity of time is a big contributing factor to feeling uncreative, particularly in our contemporary, fast paced society. Modern life can increase the struggle to carve out the time and mental space to wholeheartedly engage in creative endeavours with purpose and intention. There is an added challenge of being out of touch with the uninhibited creativity reminiscent of

Your Creative Process

childhood. Finding time to fully immerse yourself in creative pursuits can be daunting. The processes within this book can be embraced at your own pace and rhythm. Each step can be catered to your own time restraints and can be spanned over hours, days, or even weeks. You set the pace within your own boundaries and work towards building the missing connection to your own creativity.

Chapter 4

Empowering your creativity

Empowering your creativity

"All truly wise thoughts have been thought already thousands of times; but to make them truly ours, we must think them over again honestly, until they take root in our personal experience."
Johann Wolfgang von Goethe

Here, within these pages, the process itself is not breaking new ground and is not innovative. The process itself has been used and rehashed repeatedly. What is it that makes this unique? YOU make it unique. Your personal experiences, your original thoughts and questions, and your conscious and subconscious mind. I aim to empower you to harness your OWN creativity. I provide you with a comprehensive toolkit of processes and developmental techniques. I do not impose a rigid formula, but to offer you a framework for exploration and experimentation. It's your wonderfully unique, quirky, and idiosyncratic mind that holds the key to unlocking boundless creativity. I merely serve as a guide, illuminating the pathway for you to tap into that creative reservoir within yourself.

I encourage you to embrace the freedom to explore, to delve into uncharted territory, and to grant yourself the permission to experiment. It's through this journey of self-discovery and creative exploration that your true brilliance will shine.

Your Creative Process

Together, let us embark on this transformative odyssey as you discover the depths of your creative potential and unleash the full spectrum of your imagination.

Permission to take risks without fear

Experimentation is an inevitable part of life and it's a necessary step for growth and learning. Sometimes we may feel that experimentation and trying new things do not work out as we expected. But remember, it's through taking risks and pushing boundaries that we can learn what works and what doesn't. It is okay to make mistakes and experience setbacks along the journey. Perseverance will aid you in learning from the experience and use that as an opportunity for growth and development. It serves as a catalyst for personal and professional development, pushing us beyond our comfort zones and expanding the horizons of possibility. While the prospect of experimentation may sometimes evoke feelings of uncertainty or apprehension, it is through these ventures into the unknown that we uncover new insights and cultivate resilience and learn.

Recognise that failure is not a definitive endpoint, but a stepping stone on the path to success. Every misstep, every setback, presents an opportunity for learning and refinement. Through taking risks and pushing boundaries, we gain invaluable knowledge about what works and what doesn't. Each experiment, whether or not successful, contributes to our growth and understanding. Embracing the process of trial and error allows us to refine our approaches, hone our skills, and chart a course towards greater achievement.

Bravery stands as a cornerstone in the journey of creativity, a quality that empowers individuals to transcend the confines of their comfort zones and embark on daring explorations of new ideas and possibilities. The creative process demands the willingness to take risks and confront uncertainty, presenting challenges that can be both daunting and exhilarating. It is precisely through this willingness to be vulnerable that true growth and transformation occur.

By seeking feedback and engaging in constructive dialogue with others, individuals can gain valuable insights that enrich their creative journey and expand their horizons. Embracing criticism as an opportunity for learning and refinement, rather than a deterrent to progress, is a hallmark of bravery in the pursuit of creativity. By embracing bravery and pushing past fears, you will discover new insights, new opportunities and find new paths that you didn't realise were possible. Grant

Your Creative Process

yourself the freedom to take the leap, to venture into the unknown, and to embrace the possibilities that lie beyond your comfort zone. Give yourself permission to take the risk, to step boldly into uncharted territory, and to explore new horizons of creativity and possibility. Release the shackles of doubt and fear and embrace the exhilarating thrill of uncertainty. Trust in your abilities, believe in your vision, and have faith in your capacity to overcome any challenges that may arise along the way.

And so the process and journey starts...

When embarking on each step of this process, I've discovered the benefit of stepping into an unfamiliar space. For instance, if you're at home, consider entering your child's bedroom or exploring an outdoor area you rarely frequent. Similarly, if you're in your office, venture outside to a new spot. The idea is to deliberately move yourself both physically and mentally out of your comfort zone and away from your usual surroundings. While it's not mandatory, physically distancing yourself from the norm can establish a precedent before diving into the process. Alternatively, you can achieve a similar effect by mentally blocking out familiar noises or mentally detaching from your surroundings. However, I've found that physically altering your environment can be beneficial in setting the stage for the journey ahead.

According to a new study by IBM, when CEO's were asked, "What is the skill you most value in your people? [They said] Creativity, the ability to solve problems, come up with new solutions, and use brain power to figure things out."

Chapter 5

Creativity Training - Process One

Creativity Training - Process One

Convergent Mapping

*"I'm a very linear thinker so
I write beginning to end."*
Laurell K. Hamilton

Convergent mind mapping is a technique that uses a very linear map to form ideas around the subject. It is more focused and specific and works with logical ideas, regular or simple formatting and periodical process. This can be mapped as lists in order, continuous linear lines or using arrows to record the flow of logic.

There are several psychological principles that explain why convergent mind mapping can be an effective tool for organising and processing information. The human brain naturally organises information hierarchically, with more general concepts at the top and more specific details below. Convergent or linear mind mapping reflects this structure, making it easier for the brain to process and remember information. The brain is highly adept at processing visual spatial information. The linear or convergent mind mapping provides a visual representation of the relationships between ideas and concepts in a very logical manner. This can be an effective tool for organising and processing ideas and concepts.

Convergent mind mapping can be used in a variety of situations. It can be used in problem solving and developing a solution. Decision making can be used to evaluate and compare different options and weigh pros and cons. Convergent thinking can also help break down a project into manageable tasks and it can help focus on possibilities for solutions.

Convergent mapping is the use of brainstorming in a very linear manner. You start with the basis of what you need to form the idea around or the problem which you want to solve. Then you move logically through steps until you come to a final idea or a final logical solution.

It is the mapping of ideas in a logical, regular, or periodical process. Putting things down on paper in a logical order to assist your mind to formulate and solve strategically the problem at hand.

Convergent Mapping is useful when you are completely starting anew and is one of the simplest forms of mapping. It's a more natural process and can be completed in a solo environment. If you are feeling stuck or overwhelmed, this is a great step to take to loosen your mind and extend your thoughts.

Creativity Training - Process One

How to:

Start with a word or sentence. This can be any random word or something specific you want to target. As this is a linear map, I'd encourage you to draw it in a linear fashion with straight lines leading across the page. I find this gives my mind and body the sense and visual confirmation of the direction we are leaning. As you start with a word or a notion or topic, or even an object, you then draw a line in a linear direction, then add another word or notion that relates to the first. Continue in this fashion for as long as you can. Try everything you can to really open your mind to the relationship between each step, positive and negative, opposite and similar, any relative connection to the preceding step. This gives you a plethora of words or notions related to the topic, which often takes you in a logical and linear direction. If you are struggling with what to start with or just want to attempt the process, here are some ideas about what you can do to kick it off.

- Your favourite object
- Your favourite animal
- Your favourite topic
- Your favourite food or drink
- Look around the area you are currently sitting and choose an object

Your Creative Process

- The weather right now (e.g. stormy, cloudy etc)
- A feeling
- A book title
- An action

Creativity Training - Process One

BABY — TODDLER — SMALL — ANT — ARMY

FLOWERS — LEAVES — GREEN

GARDEN — HOUSE — FAMILY — SAFE — SIGN

MINES — TRUCKS — ROAD

GOLD — JEWELRY — RICH — MONEY

WRITING — LETTERS — NOTES

Your Creative Process

READING — FICTION — FANTASY — DRAGONS — WINGS — FLY — BIRDS — FEATHERS — QUILL — INK — SPLAT — MISTAKE — ERASER — DELETE — KEYBOARD — LETTERS — NUMBERS — DOUBLES — TWINS — OPPOSITE — POLAR

BOOKS — STORY — PAPER — PEN

Creativity Training - Process One

DOLPHIN		
SEA		
WATER		
DRINK		
COCKTAIL		
BAR	POWER LINES	CLOUDS
UMBRELLA	LIGHT BULB	HEAVEN
RAIN	IDEAS	STAIRWAY
LIGHTENING	INNOVATION	CLIMB
ELECTRICITY	CREATIVITY	UP
	RIGHT BRAIN	HIGH
	ART	SKY
	COLOURS	
	RAINBOW	

Your Creative Process

Assigned task:

Please take a blank piece of A4 paper and a pen (not a pencil). You are not to erase anything you write on that piece of paper. Start in the top left corner and write the word ROSE. From there, draw a small line and write a related word. Continue in this fashion around the page for 20 words. Put this paper into a folder to keep until all tasks are completed.

Chapter 6

Creativity Training - Process Two

Divergent Mapping

"Think outside the box, collapse the box, and take a f**king sharp knife to it.".
Banksy

Divergent mapping, also known as non-linear mapping, is a technique not limited to a linear, hierarchical structure. Instead, it uses a network or web of interconnected ideas with a more random connection.

The psychology behind divergent mapping is to teach you to think more broadly and freely. To consider the relationships between ideas without being limited by a predetermined structure. This allows individuals to actively and consciously think outside the proverbial square and encourages quirky solutions. The brain naturally makes connections between ideas and concepts, and non-linear mind mapping allows for a more free-flowing representation of these associations. By allowing for minimal or no connection between ideas, non-linear mind mapping can reveal previously unseen relationships between concepts. It can expose data points that deviate significantly from the general trend. It can also transform features into a space where they are more easily separable or where their relationships with the target variable are more apparent than first realised.

Your Creative Process

The concept of the left and right brain hemispheres playing distinct roles in cognitive functions has long fascinated researchers and creatives alike. The left brain is often associated with analytical thinking, logic, and rationality, while the right brain is linked to creativity, intuition, and imagination. When it comes to fostering divergent mapping, there's a metaphorical notion of coaxing the analytical left brain to 'go to sleep' to allow the more uninhibited, imaginative right brain to take the reins. This shift in dominance can lead to a state of flow where creativity flourishes and inhibitions do not exist. Ultimately, the interplay between the left and right brain hemispheres is essential for nurturing creativity. By temporarily quieting the analytical left brain and giving precedence to the imaginative right brain, individuals can unlock new realms of creative potential and bring fresh perspectives to their endeavours.

There are no hard and fast rules with divergent mapping, and that is the beauty of it. It encourages the sheer freedom, permission and encouragement to delve past your own inhibitions, your own boundaries and the boundaries you feel others put on you. This is a truly no holds bar exploration of the topic you choose with no rules.

Divergent Mapping is useful when you are more adept with other steps and really want to step

Creativity Training - Process Two

outside the norm. It's a more difficult process and does not come as naturally to most people. This is a great step to take as a solo endeavour and relax your expectation on yourself and the outcome. It aims to transport your mind far beyond the confines of reality.

How to:

Start with a word or sentence. This can be any random word or something specific you want to target. As this is a nonlinear map, I'd encourage you to draw it in a nonlinear fashion with curved lines leading all over the page or start with a word in the middle of the page and work outwards with random affair. I find this gives my mind and body the sense and visual confirmation of the random direction we are heading. My personal favourite method is to write something in the middle of the page and randomly write around the page with no thought as to location. As you jump around the page, consider the most outrageous and farther removed words to the topic or previous word.

To practice, here are some more ideas of what to start with.

- Your hobby
- Your favourite toy as a child
- Movie title

Your Creative Process

- Favourite colour
- Favourite art genre
- Favourite holiday location
- Favourite sport
- A random occupation
- Item of clothing
- Shoe brand

Creativity Training - Process Two

HANDS
FLOWER
GAME
KEY
RUG
ACT
ORB
TREE
BOATS
CHILD
FRAME
CAKE
CARS
POPCORN
MOVIE
POINTER
WORDS
BASKET

Your Creative Process

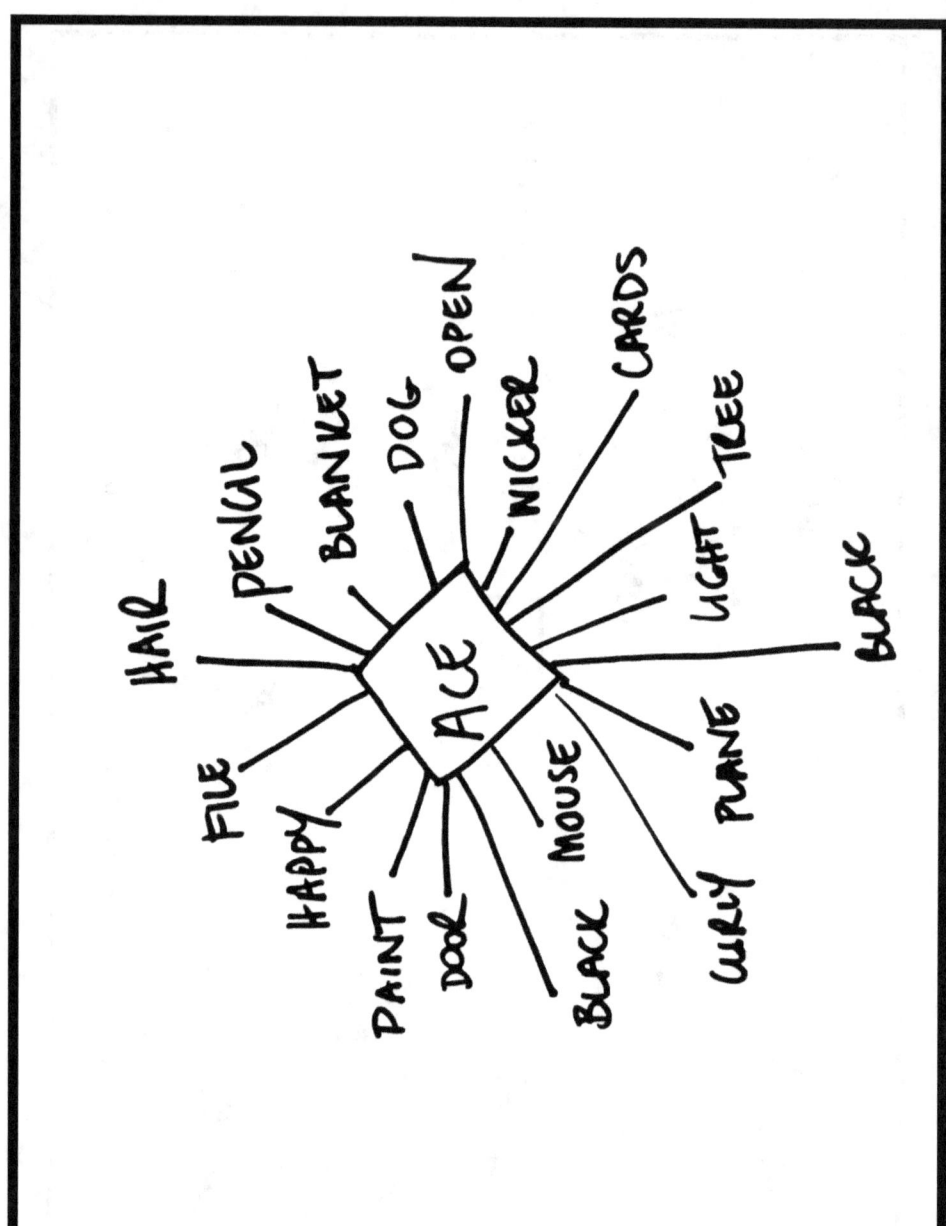

Creativity Training - Process Two

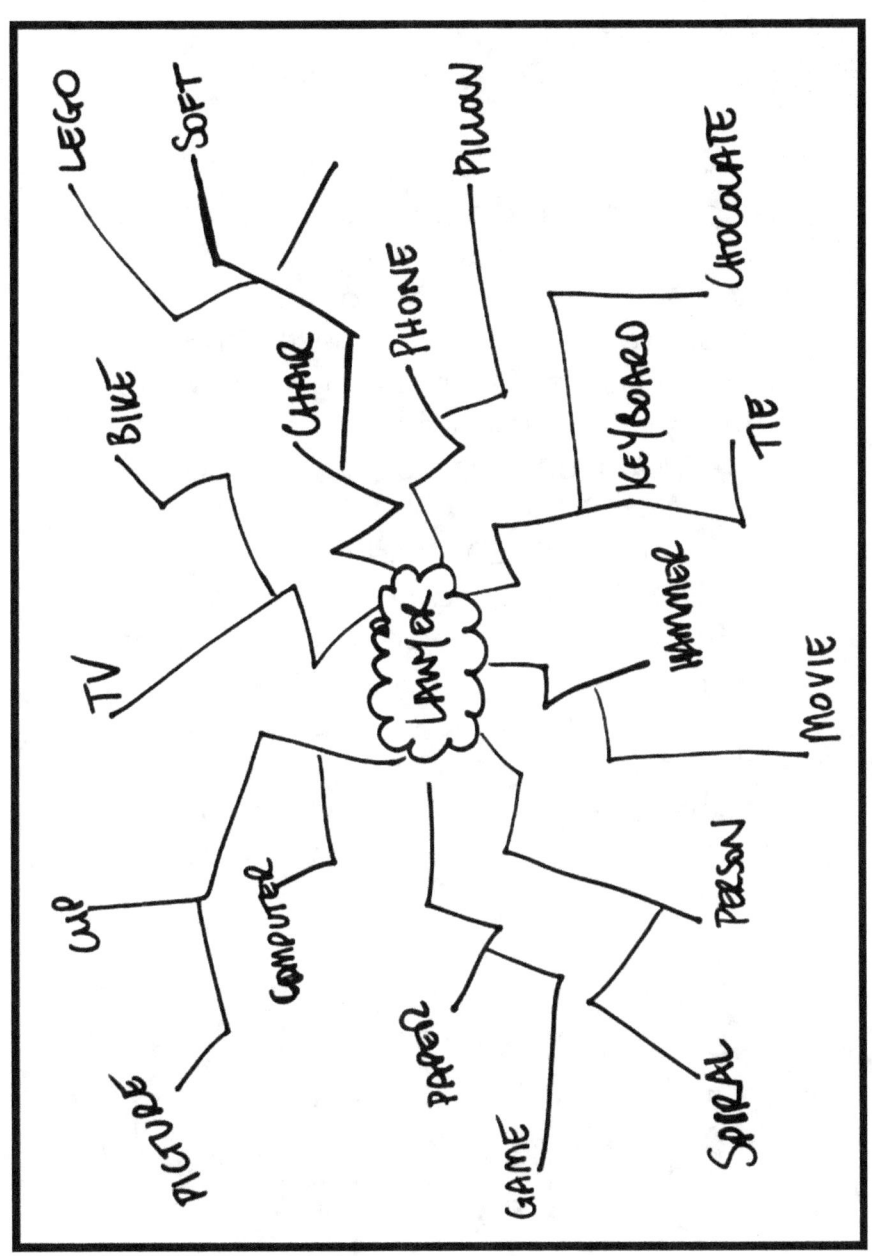

Assigned task:

Please take a blank piece of A4 paper and a pen (not a pencil). You are not to erase anything you write on that piece of paper. Move into a space that is not your norm. For example, if you are at home, go into your child's bedroom, or outside somewhere that you normally don't sit or visit. If you are in your office, go outside somewhere new. Start in the middle of the page and write the word RED. Randomly around the page, write words that have no connection whatsoever to the word RED. Forbidden words are LOVE, COLOUR, LIPSTICK, ROSE, and SANTA. Continue in this fashion around the page for 20 words. Put this paper into a folder to keep until all tasks are completed.

Chapter 7

Creativity Training - Process Three

Referencing

"Learn from many but copy none."
Mark Sanborn

Visual research is a research method that involves the use of visual materials, such as photographs, videos, and illustrations, to study social phenomena and human behavior. There are several psychological principles behind finding inspiration in visual work, which involves actively engaging with various forms of art, design, photography, and other visual mediums to stimulate creativity and generate new ideas. The human brain is highly attuned to visual stimuli. Visual referencing relies on our ability to perceive, interpret, and make sense of the visual world around us. This process involves the complex interaction between sensory organs (such as the eyes), neural pathways, and cognitive processes. It often involves recognising and identifying patterns, shapes, colours, and textures in the environment or in visual stimuli. Pattern recognition is a fundamental aspect of human cognition and plays a crucial role in tasks such as object recognition, scene analysis, and problem-solving. Visual references can trigger memories, emotions, and associations stored in long-term memory. When we encounter visual stimuli that resemble or evoke familiar patterns or experiences, our brain automatically retrieves relevant information from memory, which can influence our perception and interpretation. It also has the power to evoke emotional responses in individuals. Certain images or visual elements may elicit feelings of joy, sadness, excitement, fear, or nostalgia, depending on individual experiences, preferences, and cultural backgrounds. Visual referencing can leverage these emotional responses to convey meaning, communicate messages, or evoke specific reactions. By drawing inspiration from existing visual sources, individuals can remix, reinterpret, or combine elements in novel ways to create something new and innovative. Visual referencing allows for the exploration of different styles, techniques, and concepts, fostering a dynamic exchange of ideas and influences.

Referencing is useful when you are completely starting anew and is one of the simplest forms of research. It uses inspiration from many different locations and can be completed in a solo environment. If you are feeling stuck or overwhelmed, this step serves as an excellent catalyst for sparking new ideas.

How to:

There are multiple methods for employing referencing as a tool. If you lean towards tactile

Creativity Training - Process Three

engagement, gathering and cutting out visual references to place into a visual diary serves as an ideal option. Invest in a visual diary (a blank notebook) and assemble a collection of printed visuals, cutting and pasting them onto its pages. Convert it into a flip book, facilitating easy browsing for inspiration. For instance, when in search of concepts to evoke a particular mood or sentiment for a project, simply flip through the visual diary to uncover elements that strike a chord with you.

If you prefer digital or screen-based referencing, using platforms like Pinterest can be advantageous. Establish a board for each idea under development. Consider creating a board for the overarching idea or break it down further by dedicating a board to each component of your concept. For instance, you could curate a board specifically for capturing the mood or ambiance of your artistic composition or create one focusing on the pivotal or connecting elements for a furniture design concept. Tailor each board to suit your preferences, ranging from detailed compilations to more open-ended collections.

My personal favourite method is to assemble visual diaries of anything that inspires or excited me. I have visual diaries that date back many years that I still reference when I'm creating.

Your Creative Process

They are filled with images I've seen online, in magazines, brochures I've picked up and even my kids' drawings. Anything that has attracted me enough to pick it up or look at it twice.

Creativity Training - Process Three

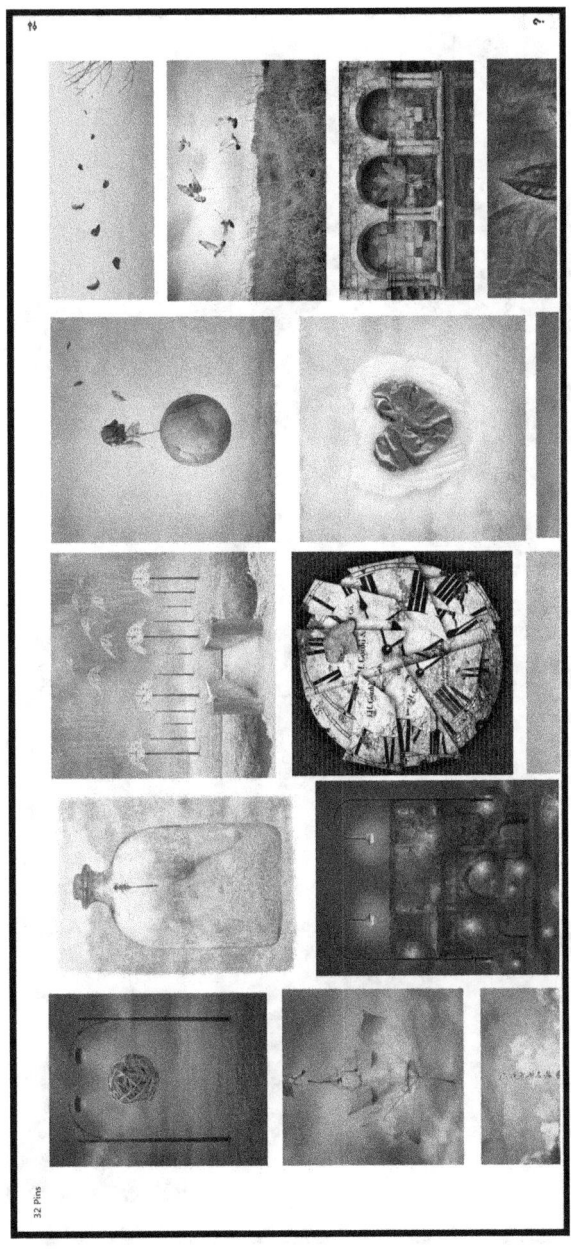

Your Creative Process

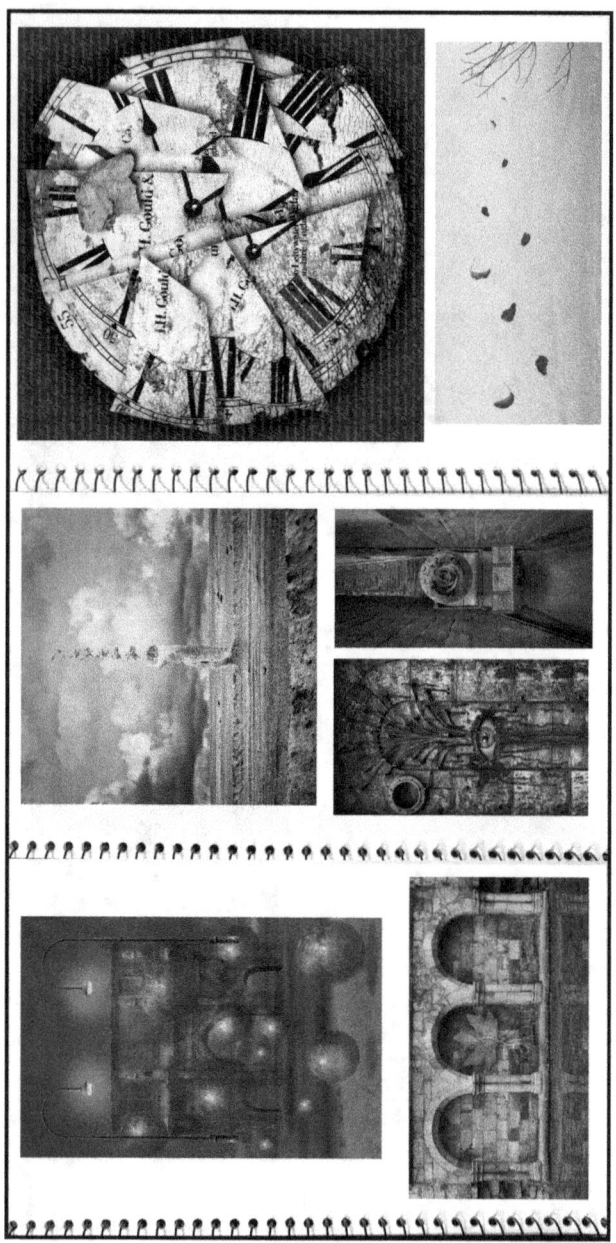

Assigned Task:
You have one of two to choose from

Tactile and Physical collection - Purchase a visual diary with blank pages, available from most retail stores. Collect any visual medium from any source and cut and paste it into the visual diary. Collection can be made from such sources as magazines, the internet (print the page) brochures, advertising materials or anything that catches your eye. When considering a topic or concept, use this as a flip book. Flip through the visual diary at a reasonable pace and see what catches your eye and resonates with you.

OR

Digital collection - Sign up to Pinterest and start a new board (or many). Search through Pinterest for visual media that excites you and relates to your topic or concept, then add it to the board. You can save boards on many topics, such as colour, style, genre, medium, anything you can think of. The more boards, the more inspiration.

Chapter 8

Creativity Training - Process Four

Creativity Training - Process Four

Visual Brainstorming

"A small idea with wings will take you higher than a big one with legs."
Matshona Dhliwayo

Visual brainstorming, also known as visual ideation or visual thinking, is a creative technique that involves using visual elements such as drawings, diagrams, sketches, symbols, and images to generate, organise, and communicate ideas. Rather than relying solely on verbal or written methods, visual brainstorming harnesses the power of visual stimuli to stimulate creativity, enhance problem-solving, and foster innovation.

In visual brainstorming sessions, participants often work collaboratively to explore and develop ideas visually. They may use whiteboards, sketchbooks, sticky notes, digital drawing tools, or other visual aids to illustrate concepts, map out relationships, and visualise potential solutions to a problem or challenge. This phase encourages free-flowing creativity, with individuals contributing their thoughts and insights through visual representations, such as sketches, diagrams, or storyboards. Visual elements are organised, grouped, or connected to identify patterns, themes, or relationships among ideas. Visual brainstorming is a versatile and powerful technique

Your Creative Process

for unleashing creativity, solving problems, and driving innovation across various disciplines and industries.

Visual brainstorming is useful when you are further into the creative process. It is a more difficult step and people tend to struggle with the fear of drawing skills. It can be a challenging fear to overcome. This is a great step to take as a solo endeavour and relax your expectation on yourself and the outcome. It aims to transport your mind far beyond the confines of reality, where drawing skills are not a necessity.

How to:

Simply sketch! The key takeaway from this approach is that you do NOT have to possess flawless drawing skills. It's about capturing shapes and embracing open representation, rather than striving for hyper-realistic renderings. Begin with a blank sheet of paper and sketch any visual elements that pertain to your subject or concept. Starting points could include doodling shapes, drafting diagrams, illustrating symbols and icons, or simply freehand doodling. There are no rigid guidelines to adhere to. Use any writing instrument - be it pen, pencil, marker, paint, or whatever is at your disposal. Incorporate vibrant colours or stick with a classic graphite pencil. There are

Creativity Training - Process Four

no constraints. Here are some ideas to get you started and remember you do not have to be able to draw these as realism. Each can be as abstract or simplistic as you like, for example, stick figures representing people. This process is to allow your right side of the brain to take over from your logical left side.

- Stick figures
- Paint splat
- Animal
- Flower
- Sports bat or ball
- Tools
- Item of clothing
- Logo you are familiar with

Your Creative Process

Creativity Training - Process Four

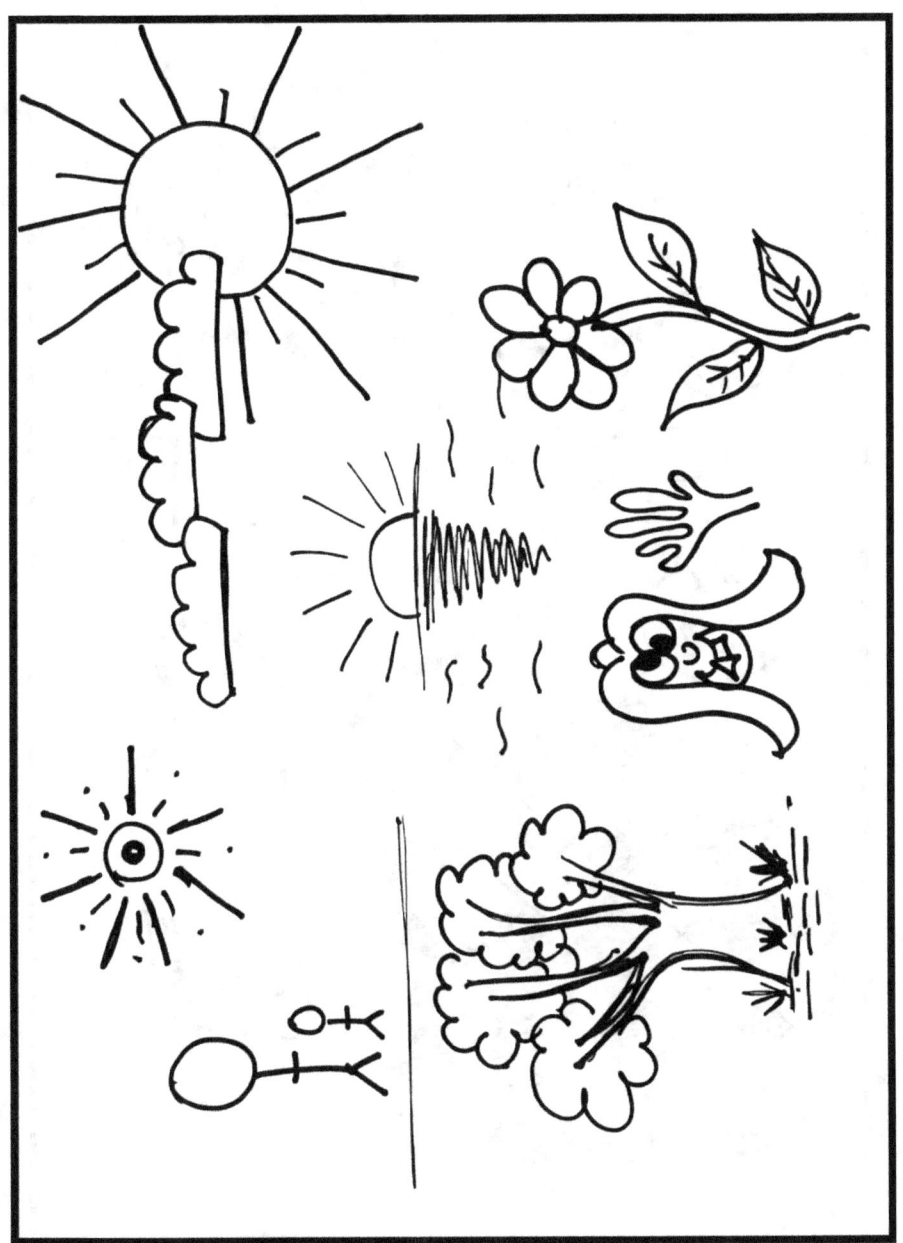

Your Creative Process

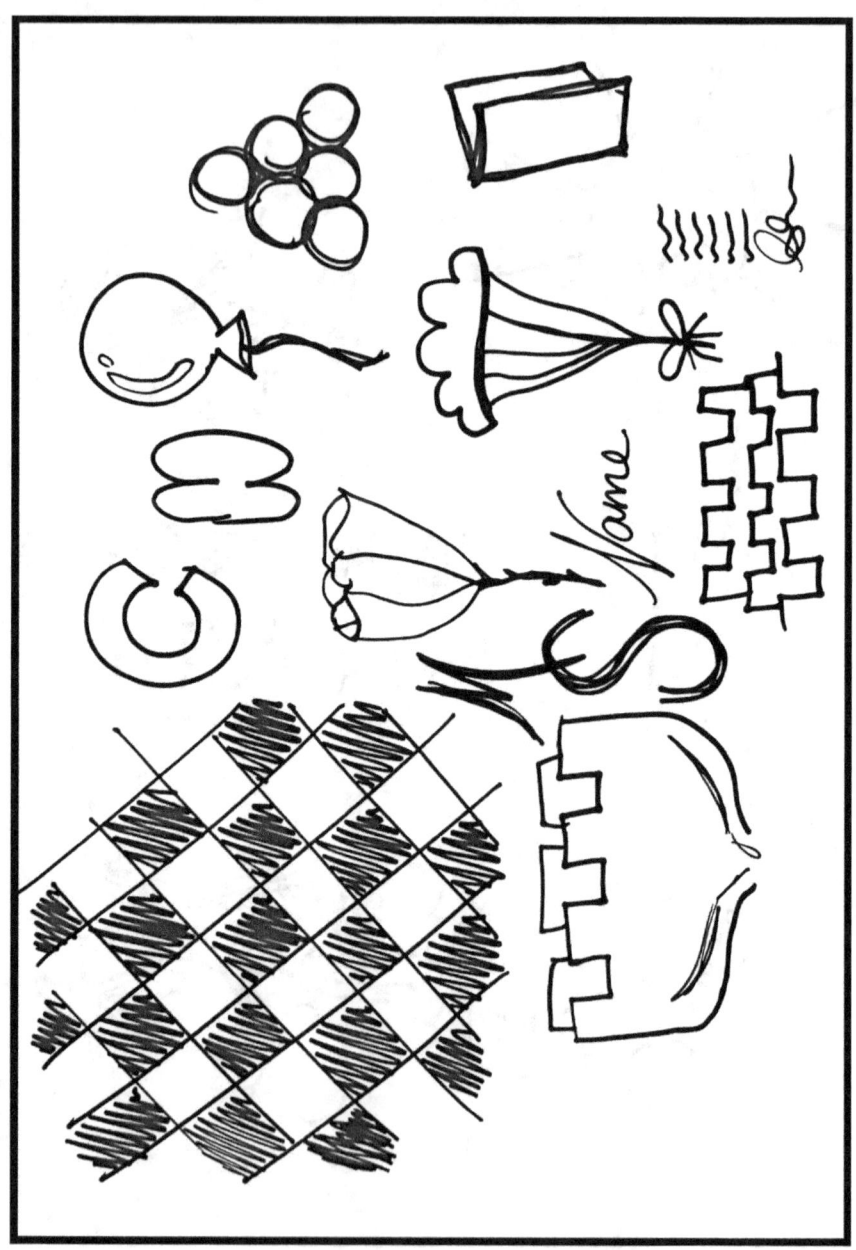

Assigned task:

Please take a blank piece of A4 paper and any drawing implement. Any sort of pen, pencil, charcoal, or paint. Again, move to a space where you are comfortable and start anywhere on the page and draw a paint splat then draw some different shapes surrounding the paint splat. Explore your own shapes and lines and use the previous pages as an example. Use different colours for each set of shapes or different thicknesses for the line work. Or even different shading. Use the space to doodle and open your mind to explore the surroundings. Even using the shapes and objects around you as inspiration, for example, leaf shapes if you are sitting outside. The outcome is a page of shapes and/or lines that can form a representation of something in the future. Put this paper into the folder to keep for the completion of all tasks.

Chapter 9

Creativity Training - Process Five

Creativity Training - Process Five

Duals

"It's easier to be creative when you've got other people to play with."
John Cleese

Duels, often referred to as verbal duels, are exchanges of verbal sparring between two individuals. These can be with single words or phrases, with each participant taking turns to push the topic further than single thought. Verbal duels can be intellectual exercises and opportunities for learning and exploration of ideas. Each participant brings their own experiences, knowledge, culture and emotions to the duel, which can really extend the boundaries of the topic far beyond a solo process. It involves generating multiple creative solutions from two different perspectives.

When verbal duels are in motion, individuals may feel motivated to perform better or generate more innovative ideas in response to the other. Seeking input from others provides opportunities for feedback and validation, which are crucial for refining and improving ideas. Positive feedback can boost confidence, motivation, and identify areas where you can contribute unique insights or expertise. Constructive critique provides the opportunity for growth, refinement, and improvement.

Your Creative Process

Collaboration fosters a collective creativity that transcends individual contributions. By combining diverse perspectives, knowledge, and skills, groups can generate more innovative solutions and overcome cognitive biases or blind spots that individuals may have when working alone.

Dueling is useful when you are starting anew and is one of the more interactive steps. It must be completed with two or more people. This step is invaluable for loosening the constraints of your mind and expanding your thoughts beyond the confines of your own world, allowing you to immerse yourself in the perspectives of others.

How to:

Hold a notepad and pen, sit opposite someone, and each of you take a turn in saying a word or phrase that relates to the topic you have chosen. As you go through the duel, write down any words or phrases that resonate with you to revisit later. Do not stop the process altogether, rather, just pause to note down the words, then continue the duel. Once you have exhausted the topic or feel the end, review the notes you have. From there, you can take those words and redo the duel, either with the same person or a different person who will bring in another perspective. Here are some ideas for topics to start with for practice.

Creativity Training - Process Five

- Your favourite animal
- Your favourite food
- Your favourite colour
- A sport
- A book title

Your Creative Process

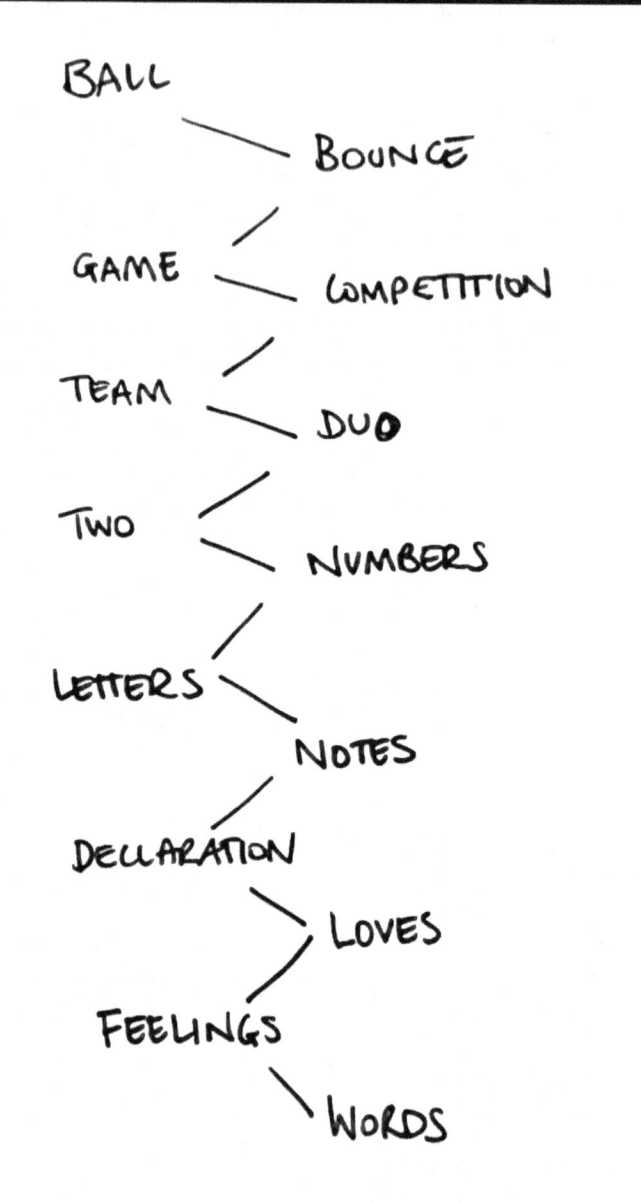

Creativity Training - Process Five

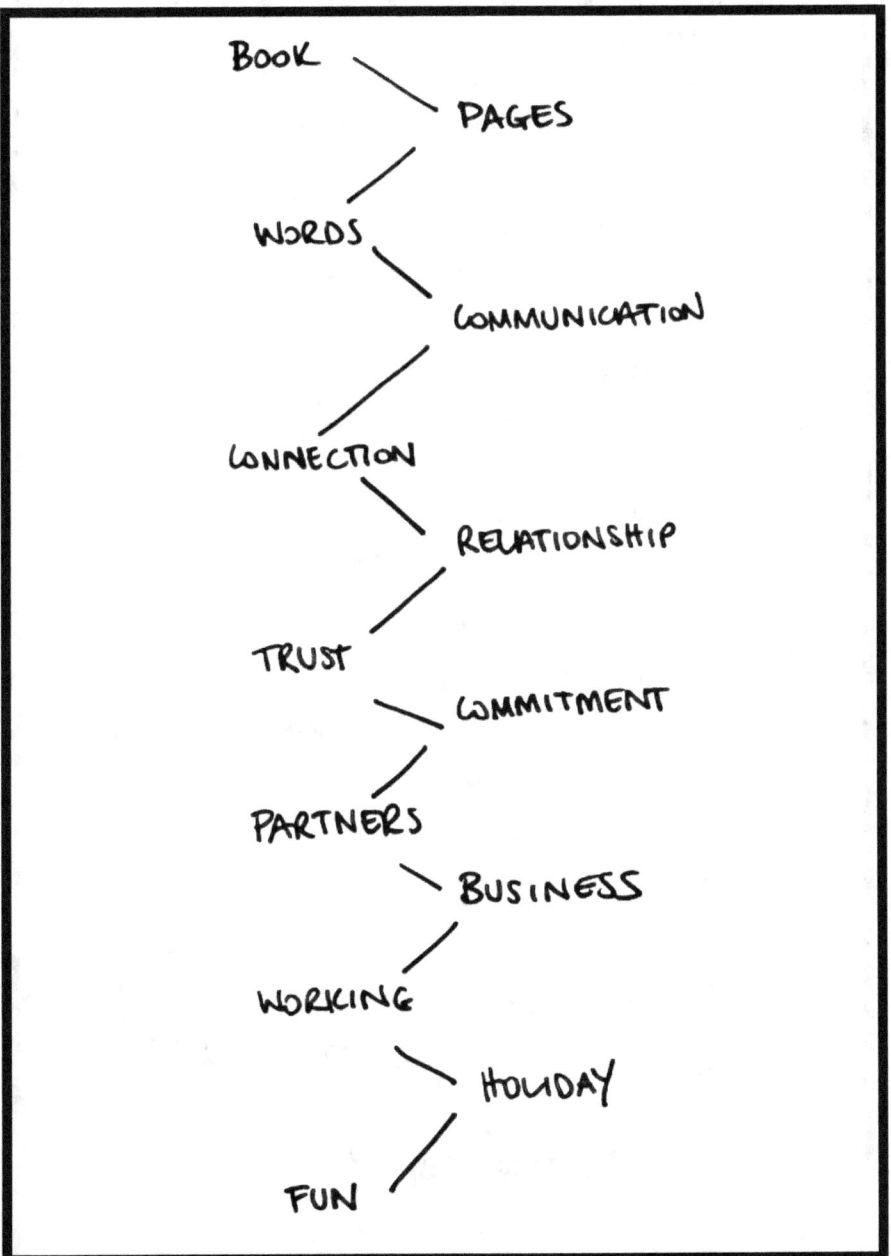

Your Creative Process

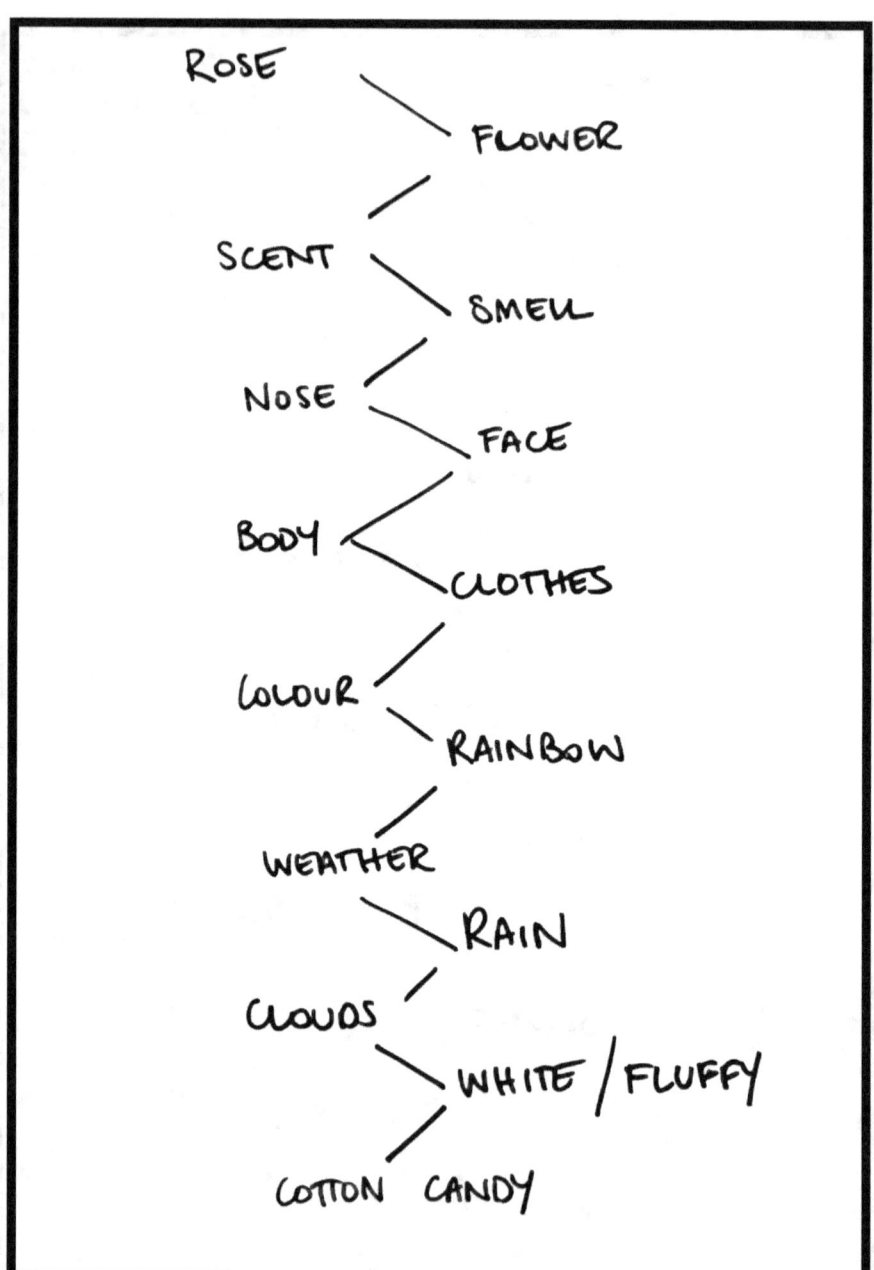

Creativity Training - Process Five

Assigned task:

Take a notepad or paper and pen. Choose a person who you would like to duel with. Each person will give you different results based on their own experiences and knowledge. You can choose a person based on the relationship you have with them, or even their perceived expertise. Sit opposite your person and explain the concept to them. Start with the word ROSE, then they say a word they feel is related to your word, or something they think of when you say your word. Then you reply with a word that relates or comes to mind once they have said their word. As you go, write down any words that are said that resonate with you. Keep that note paper and put it into the folder for when everything is complete. I would always suggest doing this with multiple people for a varied result using the same original word and see how much the wording and results vary.

Chapter 10

Creativity Training - Process Six

Creativity Training - Process Six

Combine the elements from each process

"There is no doubt that creativity is the most important human resource of all. Without creativity, there would be no progress, and we would be forever repeating the same patterns."
Edward de Bono

This is where the excitement truly begins. Having honed each of the five processes individually, you're now ready to merge them and deploy them strategically on your own creative journey. Embrace experimentation and personalise your approach. It entails blending a variety of elements, ideas, and concepts to yield a fresh, enhanced result. This improved outcome may lead you to unexplored territories that you wouldn't have discovered otherwise.

How to:

There are two options with which to combine the elements of each process. One is to mix and match as you move through the creative process. The other is to complete each process separately, then combine on completion and take portions from each to create a new concept or solution.

Your Creative Process

Combine and explore each process as a part of a whole. Stop and start as you see fit and deliberately change directions by changing the process as you go. Start collecting for your visual diary. If the mood takes you, start to doodle and draw some shapes and colours relating to your subject, then add words in a linear or nonlinear fashion to that page. Or start with the duel and study the collected words. From there, start a search online for those words and start a Pinterest board to initiate the ideas.

Combining each process upon completion of each singular process, you can expand on the concept or solution far beyond the original, while singularly concentrating on one section at a time.

Creativity Training - Process Six

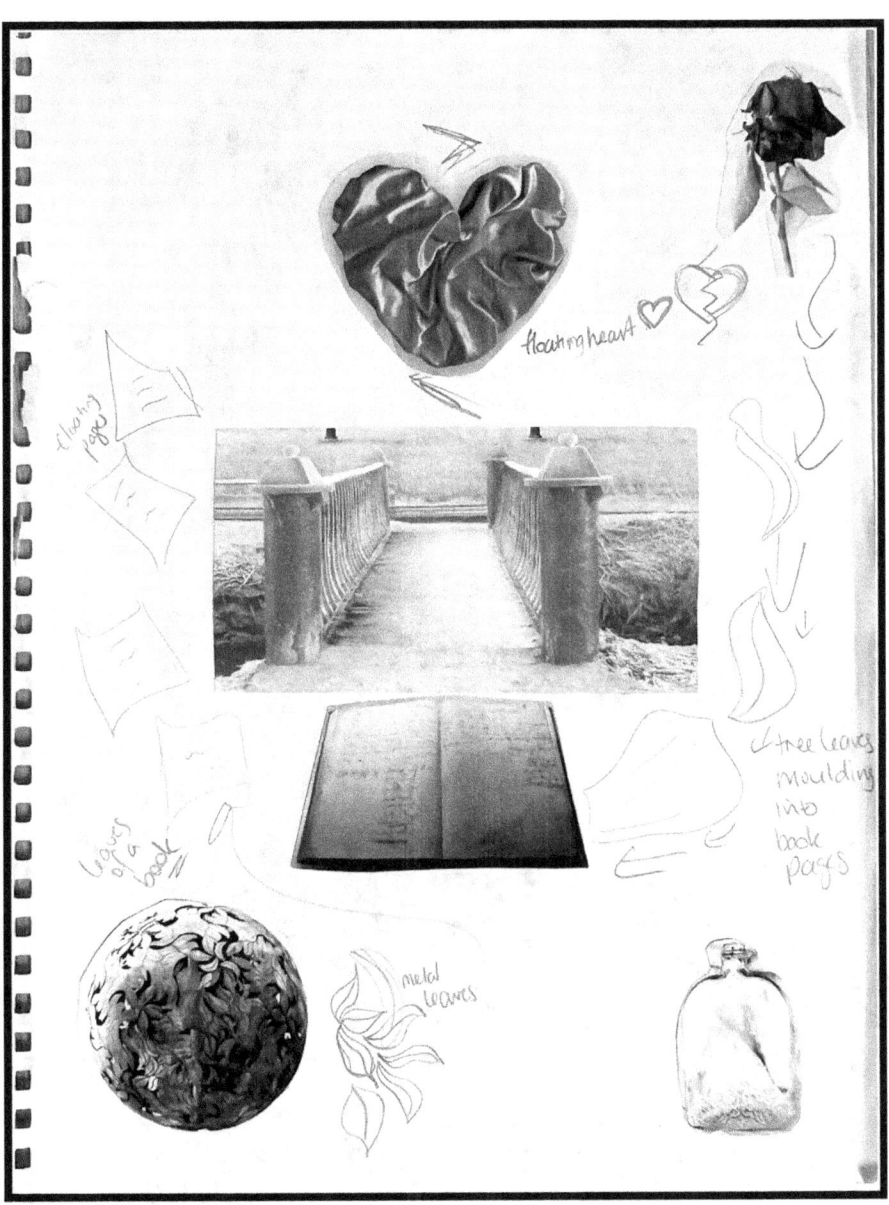

85

Your Creative Process

Assigned task:

There are two tasks associated with this module.

Firstly, start with the word ROSE. Research the word through Pinterest and print out some features that resonate with you. Cut and paste them onto a large sheet of paper. From there, please start drawing some features around the cut outs and add words that associate with what you have researched. Continue to fill the page with added cut outs, doodles and words.

Secondly, take all the information you have for completing the tasks, and combine the pieces that resonate with you to develop a concept. Refine the tasks and bring pieces of them onto a fresh piece of paper.

Chapter 11

Things to remember throughout the process

Things to remember throughout the process

There is no failure, there is feedback and learning curves, but not failure: embrace the mindset that every outcome, whether or not successful, provides valuable insights and learning opportunities. Viewing experiences this way eliminates the concept of failure and fosters continuous growth and improvements.

Take action, even when you don't feel like it: often, motivation follows action rather than precedes it. By taking steps forward despite a lack of immediate enthusiasm, you build momentum and create opportunities for progress and achievement.

Challenge your negative or non self-belief thoughts: negative thoughts can be powerful, but challenging them is crucial. Identify and question the validity of these thoughts, replacing them with more balanced and positive perspectives and pushing through the lack of self-belief. This practice helps in maintaining a healthier and more constructive mindset. It also becomes easier the more you do it.

Consciously open your mind: be intentional about embracing new ideas, perspectives, and experiences. Cultivating an open mind leads to greater creativity, adaptability, and understanding, enhancing personal and professional growth.

Your Creative Process

A change of scenery or location can really change your perspective: physical movement, such as going for a walk, travelling, or even rearranging your workspace, can provide fresh viewpoints and inspire new ideas. Changing your environment can break monotony and stimulate mental clarity and creativity. As they say, a change is as good as a holiday.

The process outlined here is not groundbreaking or innovative in itself; it has been utilised many times before. What sets it apart is your unique contribution—your personal experiences, original thoughts, and the workings of your conscious and subconscious mind. This guide aims to empower you to harness your own creativity, providing a comprehensive toolkit of processes and developmental techniques. These are not meant to impose a rigid formula, but to offer a framework for exploration and experimentation.

Your distinct, quirky, and idiosyncratic mind is the key to unlocking boundless creativity. I serve merely as a guide, illuminating the pathway for you to tap into that creative reservoir within yourself. Embrace the freedom to explore, delve into uncharted territory, and grant yourself permission to experiment. Through this journey of self-discovery and creative exploration, your true brilliance will shine.

Chapter 12

So where to from here?

So where to from here?

This book serves as a vessel, carrying you through uncharted territories of ideas, emotions, and perspectives. The voyage doesn't end upon closing the book's final pages; rather, it marks the beginning. To delve deeper into the realms of creativity and connection, you can partake in online classes and in-person workshops with me. These classes offer the invaluable opportunity to engage with fellow participants and passionate instructors, to enrich and expand upon the foundations laid in this book. Through lively discussions, practical exercises, and shared insights, these classes transform the solitary act of reading into a communal exploration, fostering growth, connection, and a deeper appreciation for the boundless wonders of creativity. To view all the options available, see www.yourcreativeprocess.com.au and like and follow 'Your Creative Process' on socials.

About The Author

Kelly Barker is a multifaceted creative force, known for her exceptional talent and passion within the world of photography. With a solid foundation in both graphic design and multimedia, as well as a Diploma in Photography, Kelly has seamlessly blended her technical expertise with her artistic vision to produce captivating photographic artwork.

Kelly's journey into the realm of photography has been marked by numerous accolades and achievements, solidifying her reputation as a respected figure in the industry. Her dedication and skill have been recognised through various awards and honours, showcasing her commitment to excellence in her craft.

Beyond her individual achievements, Kelly has also been deeply involved in shaping the photography community. Her contributions extend to her active involvement in professional organisations such as the Australian Institute of Professional Photography and Pro Photography WA. Serving on the state council of these esteemed institutions, Kelly has played a pivotal role in fostering growth and development within the industry.

In addition to her roles within professional organisations, Kelly has had the privilege of sharing her expertise as a judge in both state and national photographic competitions. Her keen eye for detail and profound understanding of the art form have made her a sought-after authority in evaluating and recognising exceptional talent.

Despite her many professional accomplishments, Kelly considers her greatest achievement to be her role as a mother to her two children. Balancing her thriving career with the joys and challenges of parenthood, Kelly draws inspiration from her family, infusing her work with a profound sense of love and authenticity.

Through her unparalleled dedication, artistic vision, and unwavering commitment to excellence, Kelly Barker continues to leave an indelible mark on the world of photography, captivating audiences and inspiring fellow creatives alike.

More Testimonials

'Kelly was extremely generous in sharing her thoughts and ideas about her creative process and the way we can all work to achieve an outcome that is sympathetic to our goals and objectives.'

Kim M

'Best workshop ever on creativity.'

Nadine H

Creative Learning Paths

Fortnightly Creative Insights

Stay informed with creative insights, curated information, interactive content and actionable advice.
Subscribe to the newsletter to receive fortnightly tips and tricks to maintain your creativity and connection.

Hands On Masterclass

There is nothing quite like learning in person. Join the hands on Masterclass and experienced teachers (facilitators) who will guide your group of likeminded people through your creative process.
Participate in real time communication, discussion and personalised attention with experienced teachers.

Online Learning

Learn in the comfort of your own home and at your own pace with flexibility, convenience and a more cost effective and accessible workshop.
Check out the options for online workshops.

www.yourcreativeprocess.com.au

www.ingramcontent.com/pod-product-compliance
Lightning Source LLC
Chambersburg PA
CBHW072101110526
44590CB00018B/3273